GRAY AND SOMETHING

ELLIOT HARMON

ISBN: 979-8-9997726-0-2
Library of Congress Control Number: 2025920879

Publisher's Cataloging-in-Publication
(Provided by Cassidy Cataloguing Services, Inc.)

Name: Harmon, Elliot, author.
Title: Gray and something / Elliot Harmon.
Description: First edition. | [Berkeley, California] :
DKW Productions, [2025]
Identifiers: LCCN: 2025920879 | ISBN: 9798999772602 (paperback)
Subjects: LCSH: Poetry. | Poetic diaries. | American poetry. |
Americana--Poetry. | Authors and publishers--Poetry. |
Litterateurs--Poetry. | United States--Intellectual life--Poetry. | Wit
and humor--Poetry. | Interpersonal relations--Poetry. | Human
behavior--Poetry. | Grief--Poetry. | Loss (Psychology)--Poetry. |
Emotions--Poetry. | Art--Poetry. | Social norms in art--Poetry. |
LCGFT: Poetry. | Autobiographies. | BISAC: POETRY / American
/ General. | POETRY / Subjects & Themes / Places. | POETRY /
Subjects & Themes / Death, Grief, Loss.
Classification: LCC: PS3608.A7483 G73 2025 | DDC: 811/.6--dc23

elliotharmon.org
Proceeds from this book will be donated to the
Electronic Frontier Foundation (eff.org).

Design & Layout by Rick Lupert
Cover Illustration by Marcus Merritt
Edited by Valerie Witte
Author Photo by Kat Cornelius

for Craig Arnold

At a bar in New York, a famous New York poet told me that my poetry was insincere. He said I built walls around myself with my poems. He placed his palm on my chest and said, "You need to write about what's in here." I said, "I'd like to think you might like it more if you saw it in the context of the full manuscript." The context of the full manuscript. Shut up.

I kept wanting to write something he'd like, to make him see me as something other than the kind of poet he thought I was. But now he's dead and somehow every night they find new things to show on TV.

Craig is dead too and every time I open Word, there aren't any.

Cast Iron Skillets Remember Everything You Cook in Them

Katie, what's
that line about any group

that would have you as a member?
I used to write poems

passports dusty and empty. Now
I only want to get

home, turn 30, check my email.
I don't even know

who's reading tonight.
I think that diner in Denver

was your idea. I think I had an omelet.
The Giants are in Pittsburgh.

We're losing. How can art
reflect life when we spend so much

of life doing art things? Everyone
I used to know is writing

poems about each other, making
jokes I don't get but laugh at.

I finally found
my Ovid, it had been behind the dryer,

the lines were dripping
out onto the wall I'm not kidding.

The ink on the cover brushed away
like seaweed with the lint.

Katie, I'm always writing
about the colors of things

under layers of other things.
I'm always wondering who visits my website.

I've started to trust ache, it's how you know
you're done stirring the polenta. You'll know

you're done with graduate school
when they take away your studio key.

jjjj

Limited

I'm going to make a gross overgeneralization here.

You're thinking of her ponytail whipping around as she turned to glance at you before she ran to catch the train, her blue bra strap dangling off her shoulder, the tank top an afterthought. You walk from the bed to the couch to the bed to the couch. You turn the TV on. You click around the Roku menu screen. She'd avoided the subject of moving together, but you didn't realize at the time that she was avoiding the subject. It was a good trick, having so many pizza coupons to talk about. You play with the remote. You play with the other remote.

She'd left her job, her home, her cat, her boyfriend. Leaving things became exhilarating; with each thing, the fantasy of not being the same person grew more palpable. She'd tried to make the idea of moving with you to Portland make sense. She'd said the words to herself as she'd done the dishes. She'd gazed out the kitchen window at the wall outside the kitchen window. Your sister had left the cat, saying, "You two need her more than I do." What did that mean even? No one ever needs a cat.

The last six sentences you remember her saying, it would occur to you much later, were all about time. And the eight weeks in toto that passed between them were more important than the words themselves. Time wasn't just the subject, you'd realize at the cafe in Quito. It was the content. Later, you'd write the six sentences to the best of your memory.

Night.

It's not too late; what's up?

I'd rather talk about this in person, but I don't know when I can get down to San Francisco.

I'm no longer sure we have the same capacity for ambiguity.

Night.

When did you guys get here?

Once she's settled into the sleeper car and the train's pulled out of Oakland, she hangs her coat up on the coat rack. That makes it feel real, makes the room hers. Years before, she wrote a story about a woman who just doesn't go home on September 11, stops using her bank account, moves into a hotel. She'd gotten the idea from a post she'd seen on Metafilter, someone who'd supposedly done that. But in her version, the hero keeps meeting the same kinds of people and getting the same kinds of jobs she had before, as though the life she'd wanted to escape was inevitable. Upon reflection, the story embarrassed her: *Sorry about losing your loved ones, everybody. I can sympathize. My life is so predictable.* She digs in her purse for a pack of cigarettes. You can't smoke on the train, but she wants to be ready for the first stop. She pulls out two pizza coupons and drops them in the little garbage can.

He notices her during the smoke break—superficially, that she's the most attractive person on the train, male or female. But also that she's so visibly uncomfortable on it. She sprints out the door the moment they open it. When they shout for people to get back onboard, she doesn't even seem to hear them. That night, somewhere in Utah, he'll be lying on his back playing a game on his phone. He'll be startled when he sees he has a signal. He'll try to think of people he can text that time of night. He'll check Reddit. He'll watch 10 minutes of a show on Netflix before the signal drops. He watches out the window—she finally climbs onboard just before they shut the door.

The next day, he slips a note under her door: "I have beer and whiskey to finish before we get to Chicago. Come to my room if you want some. This is not creepy." At the bar in Chicago, she'll tell him, "You know that saying 'this is not creepy' made it creepier." When the nachos arrive, she'll say, "Give me one of those cheese pills." He feels foolish upon letting go of the note, but not as foolish as he'd feared he would.

In her room, she turns the note around in her fingertips. She unfolds it, folds it the other way along the crease, so that his words are on the outside. She unfolds it. She writes a list below his note:

spelt bread
cage-free eggs
USB cable?
easily accessible marijuana
having my own bedroom

You open the refrigerator. You find half a loaf of her bread shoved in the back. You take it out, and a thing of grape jelly. You check the bread for mold. You walk out onto the front steps. "Spelt still has gluten," you'd told her. "You should just eat more normal things." She was still mad about the thing with her mom. She said, "Just," and went back to playing 2048. The wind tips over a trash can; it rolls down the hill until it hits a light post. You go back inside. You check the bread for mold.

"I'm going to make a gross overgeneralization here," he starts out. She cuts him off and says, "Just go for it," recognizing him as the kind of guy who says things like "I'm going to make a gross overgeneralization here" all the time. "Okay," he says. "It seems like everyone our age can barely afford rent. And so money plays a larger role than it should in all of our major life choices. Like where to live and who to be in a relationship with." She says, "That's been really true for me." Later, he'll wonder if she thought he wanted to have sex with her, and if she wanted to. He'll wish he had her email address, so he could not ask her.

I *did* know it would make it creepier, Megan. But I thought pretending not to know would make it easier.

I've Never Had a Porch Before or Since

2002

It was the end of
that summer when it took all morning
to watch a beer commercial,
when the radio kept pointing out

the best sundresses. Well shit,
A, all I wanted
was to pick leaves off your jacket,

to watch you brush your teeth, and so
I waited on the porch, counted leaves,
and counted leaves. I've never had
a porch before or since.

1998

We were young enough that smoking
was still a matter of aesthetics
and you rocked it, dude.

You lifted it to your lips
and opened your Zippo
in one fast motion, with
one hand. I wanted

to be a part of that performance.
I wanted in your van.

2000

We said names of authors to
each other but

objectively, K,
we were pretty dumb.

We didn't know that
knowing names of things is

not knowing things.
But one time in Montana,

I walked up behind you, said
your name, you

didn't even turn around. You
grabbed my hands

and held them to your breasts. I
remember that shit.

2001

I remember when we bought
a broken *Mouse Trap* game
at the thrift store—

we went there during
the couple hours that afternoon
when it wasn't snowing,

walking on the tire tracks
because the sidewalk was too icy.
25¢ SOME PIECES MISSING

The game didn't matter;
we only wanted what anyone
would want—to bring the machine

to health. We found simulacra
for the missing pieces—
a *Star Wars* figure for

the diver; for the boot,
a plastic fork with pennies
taped to it. It never happened.

We pretended. When the marble—
maybe it was too big for
the slide?—got stuck again

and we were sick of engineering,
you just pushed it
down yourself

and we high-fived. I remember
kissing you, first on your cheek
and then your mouth,

not sure which was correct. And
the sunlight in the morning, how
bright it made the snow.

2003

Sitting with you on your
kitchen floor drinking your

coffee
was better than ice cream

or watching the election
results.

It was better than WrestleMania
or finishing a hard sudoku.

It was better than
when Canada geese

land all over town
and block the roads and everyone

just sits there in their cars.

Gray and Something

I think I wrote this in
2004:

I bought a shiny
black cable

so I could listen
to your voicemails
in amazing surround

but it didn't work.

You did this poem at the haiku slam in Omaha, something like, "My cat is gray and hungry / like life without you." I think about that all the time, the literal gray and literal hungry, the figurative hungry and figurative gray. But I'm never sure if it was hungry. It was gray and something.

Just last year it was about interweaving communities for social change but now they're like in Alabama running a chicken truck, Instagramming videos of themselves talking about their chicken in voices that seem maybe racist? I don't get it, but *I've* never been paid to make anything tangible in my life. I don't like knowing there are mice here either. But you know.

The most successful writer in my master's program was the least congenial. Your cornbread was the thing that I enjoyed the least self-consciously today. My greatest fault is my belief that records make me interesting, but you can likely think of greater faults. It's not jealousy, it's something else.

When you told me that leaving me at that Greyhound station in Tacoma and walking away from me felt like the most unnatural thing you'd ever had to do. I always remind you of that when we fight. And I always think it will make you stop being mad; is that naive? It never works.

And then there was the refrigerator door full-on coming off of the fridge two days before Christmas. It was too funny to be a punchline, after the MRI and the CT scan and Coronavirus and police brutality. It slows your thoughts to one-at-a-time. *How do you fix this? Does anyone fix it? Should I unplug it? Will the president try to stop the inauguration? Are the cranberries even still good?* Or it wasn't funny enough.

I'm scared my altitude sickness will become a thing you resent me for.

Notes Taken in Research for a Poem About *Ms. Pac-Man*

It wasn't even a real Namco game, I learn
from Googling. It was a bootleg. A better, tougher *Pac-Man*
made by hackers. Instead of suing, Namco bought the rights.

We're made to understand the female Pac-Man was key:
A circle wearing a bow, a female circle.
The McDonald's toys were pink, the color of girl-toys.

.

I ask Kathleen about it over coffee. "That's dumb,"
she says. *"Let's make the exact same game, except
with a bow in Pac-Man's hair. The girls will love it."*

She also has lipstick, in fairness, and a beauty mark,
and eyes. You could argue she is gendered
and her predecessor, the featureless

yellow circle, is androgynous. But no,

.

no, Pac-Man must be male. Though I believed,
incorrectly, for as long as I knew something existed called a pacman

frog, that the frog existed first. The ghosts, never identified
as ghosts: Inky, Pinky, Blinky, and Clyde

become their female forms: Inky, Pinky,
Blinky, Sue. The female ghosts are
more sporadic, uncontrollable, more dangerous.

.

There's a sound, like some electric siren, that permeates
Ms. Pac-Man. The sound of dots being swallowed? But no,
it still goes on when she's not moving. Marc says
he thought it was just the sound *Ms. Pac-Man* makes.
Meaning not the character, the game.

.

More than your hair or brushing your hair, I miss
your ability to estimate sines and cosines,
your high *Ms. Pac-Man* scores, your blanket.
I can't even find any of the records

you always played, let alone you.
Like a siren, or maybe someone saying
"Wow wow wow," the game forever shocked
that it exists. Or the sound of ghosts.

.

I do not know which to prefer,
the beauty of pursuit
or the beauty of denouement,
the last dot in *Ms. Pac-Man*
or just after.

.

In a YouTube video, a thirteen-yr-old boy beats three levels
of *Pac-Man* blindfolded, following one path repeatedly,

increasing speed. The ghosts go where they must. Is that how
we know they're *ghosts*, never being told by anyone,
and not the *monsters*

they're numbly labeled by instructions?
You couldn't do that in *Ms. Pac-Man*,
there's randomness and gender,

the humanness of ghosts unquestionably real,

the chorus relentlessly chanting, "Wow."
Your emails come at the worst times. Damnit,
can't you see I'm trying to be domestic?

.

Each note an invitation to cantilever words
along the interstate and frankly,
I just burned my wife's breakfast.
"Well, what about you? Would you rather control

a female character?" She shakes her head.
"I really don't like those games."

.

Unlike *Pac-Man*, *Ms. Pac-Man* hints at plot,
with a crude animation every two levels.

Act 1: *They Meet.* Serendipitously a cartoon heart
is called into existence just above their heads.

Act 2: *The Chase.* Pac-Man chases Ms. Pac-Man
across the screen. Ms. Pac-Man
chases Pac-Man across the screen.

Act 3: *Junior.* A stork drops a baby
on the Pac-Man, who shares his father's indescriptness

.

but nothing is resolved. The acts repeat indefinitely.
There could be a joke about that, but
this isn't really that kind of thing.

Actually, Marc tells me, it does end. Around
level 150 the processor crashes,

.

so there is that.

For so long I believed that everyone
was lonely, poetry the only hope
for tiny slivers of connectedness.
It turns out I was wrong, it was
just me. But here,

.

I stall the ghosts until they're
crowded in the corner, I wait
to eat my dot and strike. "What's
that noise?" she asks. "It's just

the game," I say. She's carrying
the mail, her reflection
on the screen reluctantly snaps
into focus as she opens the blinds.

The Dogs Are in the Enclosed Pool Area. Garage Side Door Is Open.

June 25, 2007

One

On the day they found you, Disneyland

shut down *It's a Small World,*
but only the music and the lights. People

watched, stunned, the doll children dance
to the hum of their own motors

and splashing water, lit only
by the faint, red exit sign. So popular,

extra line-holding ropes were flown in
from Hong Kong. Cast members

have been told to contravene. Sometimes
they answer, "We were closed that day."

Two

On the day they found you, a teenager

across the street had written on my car,
SO MATERIAL A DIFFERENCE DOES IT MAKE,

NOT WHAT ILLS ARE SUFFERED, BUT
WHAT KIND OF MAN SUFFERS THEM.

The milkman said, "I heard they're gonna
Photoshop him out of the tapes, just like

the old logo." I said, "I don't think that's funny."
He said, "You want this milk or not?"

I sat on the front step and drank
the full bottle, watching *The Price Is Right*

through the neighbors' window.
I haven't mentioned the graffiti yet.

Three

On the day they found you, fat weathermen

in no less than nine major cities
forewent their presentations altogether

to perform Schoenberg's *A Survivor
from Warsaw* a capella. Each insists

it dawned on him to do so at the moment,
but was not surprised about the others.

Only one anchor, in Cincinnati, tried
to stop him. She's been graciously

transferred to a mailroom at a partner station.
I read on Wikipedia that Naxos

was compiling an album, but I can't find that
anymore. It might have been a prank.

Four

On the day they found you, my football coach

was voiceless. Having tried in vain
to draw some Xs on the chalkboard,

he put down the chalk
and watched us breathe. I thought

I saw him mouth, "I'm sorry."
Finally the quarterback stood up,

picked up the chalk, and scribbled
integral formulas. First the basic ones

from college, then some tougher ones.
He'd fill the board and quickly smear it

with his arm and start again, until the board
was only a large, white, dusty rectangle.

Five

On the day they found you, priests

gave their flocks choke holds and the tooth fairy
gave my niece *No Way Out 2006*. She told me

that she would be a wrestler when she grew up.
I didn't tell her it had been the day

I'd finally stopped wanting to grow up
and be a wrestler, but Chris, I did give her

a suplex and locked her leg until she tapped,
almost in tears from laughter.

Six

On the day they found you, I

couldn't even think of anyone
to call, so I watched some matches

online. They'd Photoshopped
you out, just like the old logo, so HHH

writhed in your invisible arms,
and when he finally tapped, they played

your music and the crowd around
the empty ring chanted bleeps.

Satan Is Real

1

This poem shares its title with the Louvin Brothers'
1959 record, a pivotal work

in country gospel with the most embarrassing-
ly bad album art in music history.

On the cover stand the Louvins midsong, smiling,
arms outstretched, apparently in hell,

an awkward, naked, buck-toothed Satan looms behind.
He sure doesn't look very real in the photo.

Carla punches me. "Shut up," she says. "It's okay
if it looks dumb. No one was arguing." Today

I'm driving my friend Carla to South Dakota,
for the funeral of her Uncle Irving, who,

the newspaper said, suffered a fatal accident
while cleaning his shotgun, preceded by his wife

with liver problems. Her only friend who drives,
I got the job. While she's in White Lake,

I'll be in Rapid City with some people.
The reason for the title, among other things,

is that Carla knows the album from her girlhood
White Lake vacations. She'd find the record—

perhaps the goofy Satan allured her—and beg,
demand, to hear it again. We're in Durango,

CO, one of those cheapass motels off
the interstate, you park the car outside your room

and pick up towels at the desk. The VACANCY
hums and flickers just like in cartoons, I hear it

even with the TV on. I'm tired—driven
in a rented car all day. Except for Carla's

iPod—a playlist she'd compiled for the trip
mercilessly labeled "Middle America"—

it was mostly silence. During the fourth time through
Satan Is Real, as four billboards with aborted

fetuses flew by—like a Burma-Shave jingle,
except with fetuses—she turned to me and said,

"The farther you get from the ocean, this music
gets less fun," clicking through the playlist for

something less specific. Now, we're sinking
into our $29/night bed—

at any other time, this would be awkward—
emptying the cheapest bottle of red wine

from the all-night grocery, keeping an eye on
the religious channel. They're showing that one guy

with the whiteboards, who knows Hebrew, Latin, Greek,
and runs across the stage, a different marker each.

He's teaching on the shades of meaning of the word
"cleanse," a toll-free number never leaves the screen,

in case the lecture stirs the need to pray. "What does
'Selah' mean?" Carla asks. I say, "Maybe *nervous*

laughter." She says, "Maybe it means 'I guess.'" Silence.
"Cleaning his shotgun," she almost laughs. "It's okay,

I didn't really know him. I mean I did..."
The professor switches pens, jogs from Hebrew back

to English. She fiddles with the volume, turns away
to see the show's reflection in the window. "I don't know,"

she says. "I guess I did."
She tells me of his prayers at dinner, and the dirt

which sometimes hid, but never left his fingers,
how he seldom opened the church hymnal,

though he sang the real bass part, the printed one
that no one ever sings. Again she plays with the remote.

"What about after your aunt died?" I venture. She says,
"I think he was pretty lonely before she died, too."

I pour the final drops into my stained red
plastic cup as the whiteboards

darken with variations of cleansing,
muted, and my friend brushes her teeth.

2

It was common, midway through his songs, for Ira Louvin to insert a prose block, a miniature sermon, though he never preached onstage.

The album's title cut features such a monologue, in which an old man begs a preacher not to deny the existence of evil, because as wonderfully present as the Lord may be, Satan is real too. "For once I had a happy home," Louvin recites. "I was loved and respected by my family. I was looked upon as a leader in my community. And then—Satan came into my life."

It's funny. It's forced, and it's hard not to laugh, at least a little. And perhaps it's that awkwardness, that need to snicker, that's caused the recent surge in popularity for the Louvins and acts like them.

In truth, is it even the same album it was when they recorded it? It's a reprint, 2001, coastal, still in cellophane. Satan, a brighter shade of orange, protected by fluorescent bulbs in record shops Ira would have been embarrassed to enter, and vice versa.

It's worth noting that Ira built Satan himself. He freehanded it on a piece of plywood. The burning rocks, the fire, they're all real, staged in a junkyard outside of town. But the photograph seems so fake—so obviously photoshopped, not aspiring to be anything but photoshopped—that when you find out it isn't, you might half wonder why he went through all the work. But then, you also know. Maybe you know.

There's a jokiness in Ira's music, or something like jokiness. Hesitating a bit behind the beat, as if to say, again and again, it's just a song. It's not a style of singing, exactly; it's an affectation, one that could be applied to any genre. Stephin Merritt does it; so did Billie Holiday. Of course Johnny Cash sang like that, but only in the murder songs. Why would someone sing a God song that way?

Ira was Elvis Presley's favorite songwriter. He said that the Louvins were his heroes and that touring with them was the highlight of his career. After a show, Presley was backstage playing gospel on an old piano, as he had many times before. Ira could no longer take the contradiction—what seemed a contradiction in his mind, between the onstage Presley and this one—and he called Elvis the n-word.

That was how Ira worked. He ended his relationships all at once, like tearing off a Band-Aid. His wife, his brother Charlie (who still will play a gig or two of Ira's songs), his other wife, himself.

3

It was good to drive the other way, in truth;
the unoffensive backsides of the billboards,

the green signs heralding familiar towns
we've slept on couches in. "You know what else they found?"

you said. "A shoebox full of swimsuit magazines."
You shook your head in feigned embarrassment.

"He couldn't even buy real porn." I laughed,
though it was pretty dreary. The same roadside motel,

but a room across the hall and better booze,
religious channel only playing crappy music,

so I turned the dial to find better
crappy music. I didn't listen at the time

to what you told me about the funeral.
I nodded, and I maybe even smiled,

but I didn't hear it 'til the next afternoon,
in the endlessness of Wyoming,

when you were fluctuating between sleep
and the gospel music book I'd gotten you

in Rapid, your skirt and fingernails the silly
red-orange color—but sexy—of fake Satans.

I thought of it then, how there was no sadness
at the service, the chubby crying aunts

you only know as chubby crying aunts.
It was the dinner afterward, you'd said,

the laughter that betrayed what it was meant to hide,
the grapes suspended in red jello, your stepmom

earnestly discussing gun safety. And you knew,
you'd told me, that you were one of the sad

smiling people. You knew that just like you, each line
they sang of "Victory in Jesus" without

flinching was a quiet victory. And you
were slightly less alone.

Wyoming just kept coming, one big deck
of mile markers, cracks in pavement the only sound.

One little out-of-place cloud in the sky, a truck
so far ahead of us it might not be there.

And then there's that album. And perhaps,
it struck me as I zigzagged down I-80

fumbling to find it on your iPod,
this is the piece of evidence you wish

you hadn't found, the dented car in the lot
you long to abandon. You want to

throw it back in the pile—cover it with
Cash Sings Gospel,

curse your childhood self for outing it. Not the gun,
not the medical report, not the bottles,

this proves it was that way for Irving too;
like all relationships with God or anyone,

his was a relationship with doubt,
each prayer fought, each stilted smile a victory.

The book was on your lap, open to the part
where Ira dies, drunk, driving, three bullets

in his chest remain from his wife a year ago,
and it's not even a surprise. Hell, look at him,

smiling like he's singing at the county fair
in Hell, the silly Satan in the background

begging to be a joke. Yeah, Satan is real.
He's the only real thing in that photo. *Utah:*

Life Elevated, says the sign. "How long
was I asleep?" you whisper. I say, "I don't know."

You ask me to pull over at the rest stop,
so I lean against the car and watch a squirrel

barrel across the highway neither avoiding
nor hitting the trucks. A tourist family

haggles over seat arrangements, the young boy
fiddles with his shorts. It barely starts to rain,

the Canada geese far overhead shout
at themselves and each other. Cicadas.

I lie back on the hood—this last good night
of summer—and watch, listen, and slowly wait.

Afterword

Elliot Harmon was our friend. When he passed away at age 40, our grief was amplified by the fact that Elliot was relatively young and extremely engaged with a wide range of projects; his tireless creative energy was a gift that the world needed—still needs. We knew he had more to give. So at the request of Elliot's wife, Kat, we took on the daunting task of editing and publishing his last known poetry manuscript. In the beginning, it was difficult and painful to focus so intently on the work of a person we missed, a person who left too soon, who should have been alive to approve our edits. Our early editorial meetings were somber occasions. But as the project progressed, something beautiful happened: We started having fun. We got excited about creative ideas for marketing the book; how we would design the cover; and an idea, in progress, called "the 100 voices of Elliot Harmon," which would be a series of readings where friends would read excerpts from this book, giving new life to his words. As we worked on the project of this book, we asked questions leading to stories about Elliot, such as a memory of a time when he expressed a very strong opinion about an apostrophe or his suggestion of a "cold open" for a book he edited. At times, it felt as if Elliot was there with us, on the Zoom calls, and he had simply stepped offscreen for a while.

Our intent as editors and publishers was to produce the book Elliot would have wanted. We leaned heavily on a document saved on his computer entitled "the 2019 manuscript for reals." We knew that changes had been made to the poems in this "final" document, so we used primary sources to create a timeline to inform the revisions we knew he had made in his lifetime. Sources included a recording of a Zoom poetry reading Elliot hosted on April 24, 2021 (posted on YouTube with the title "VAX PARTY USA - Literary vaccine celebration"); a pdf called "what I'm going to read next Saturday"; a series of email exchanges between Della, Jessica, and Elliot, in which we discussed edits to a portion of the manuscript that was to be published in Jessica's journal, *Monday Night;* the final version of the poems, approved by Elliot, that appeared posthumously in issue 24, published on December 5, 2021; and Elliot's website, elliotharmon.org. We also relied on our own memories of Elliot's stated preferences and Kat's guidance. What we present here is our best attempt at staying true to Elliot's voice and vision.

Sincerely,

Heidi Kasa
Della Watson
Jessica Wickens
Mike Young

About the Author

Elliot Harmon was a poet. Early in his career, Elliot received a degree in English from the University of South Dakota and was active in the Midwest arts community. He wrote and directed plays and became an integral part of the slam poetry scene. In San Francisco, Elliot attended California College of the Arts, where he received an MFA in creative writing. He ran literary readings; edited the online poetry journal *Idiolexicon;* and started his own press, Mission Cleaners. Along with his work as a poet, Elliot advocated for free speech and the right to innovate online as the Activism Director for the Electronic Frontier Foundation. Elliot's passions were as varied as his career—from professional wrestling to country music to French New Wave cinema. Elliot lived with his wife, Kat, and their cat, Nora. The title of this book, *Gray and Something*, is a reference to said cat. Elliot died of melanoma on October 23, 2021, in his home in San Francisco. Elliot is remembered by his coworkers, friends, and family as a smart, kind, generous, and thoughtful person.

Notes

P.9: One of the great mysteries of this book is the presence of the four j's. Given the formatting, it seems that "jjjj" is the title of a poem that consists of a blank page. Or, it could have been a placeholder; a typo; or his cat, Nora, stepping on the keyboard.

P. 42: This poem is based on a text message that read, "The dogs are in the enclosed pool area. Garage side door is open." Elliot wrote this note on first publication and on his website: "The title is a text message Chris Benoit sent a neighbor shortly before his death. The poem is an elegy where an elegy is not possible."

P. 48: We had to make editorial choices that may differ from what Elliot and an editor would have worked out. One example is "embarrassing-/ly," which was his original line break. Though the hyphen and the line break appear awkward, we believe this was intentional and that this is how Elliot would have read the poem aloud.

P. 53: Regarding the incident between Ira and Elvis using language that many people find inappropriate today, we consulted other sources and feel this is somewhat a case of historical reporting. If you'd like to learn more, here's an article describing the complexities of the altercation. chicagoreader.com/music/spiritualized

P. 56: Elliot's original manuscript includes *Cash Sings Gospel,* and our copy editor couldn't find that album listed but found other similarly titled albums.

Acknowledgments

Thank you to the following journals for prior publication of these poems:

"Satan Is Real," *Beeswax Magazine* and *Killing the Buddha*

"The dogs are in the enclosed pool area. Garage side door is open." *Sorry for Snake*

"Notes Taken in Research for a Poem About *Ms. Pac-Man*," *DIAGRAM*

Selections from "Gray and Something," *Monday Night*

We would like to thank Valerie Witte for copy editing and proofreading this manuscript, Marcus Merritt for creating the cover illustration, and Rick Lupert for book layout and design. Thank you to all of Elliot's family and friends who supported him in his myriad personal and professional pursuits, and to those who published very meaningful remembrances and made beautiful artwork in his honor. Thank you to Elliot's wife, Kat Cornelius, for preserving his work and memory by making this book happen.